Charles W. Shields

The Directory for Public Worship and the Book of Common

Prayer

considered with reference to the question of a Presbyterian liturgy

Charles W. Shields

The Directory for Public Worship and the Book of Common Prayer
considered with reference to the question of a Presbyterian liturgy

ISBN/EAN: 9783337291860

Printed in Europe, USA, Canada, Australia, Japan

Cover: Foto ©Lupo / pixelio.de

More available books at **www.hansebooks.com**

THE

DIRECTORY FOR PUBLIC WORSHIP

AND

THE BOOK OF COMMON PRAYER.

THE

DIRECTORY FOR PUBLIC WORSHIP

AND

THE BOOK OF COMMON PRAYER,

CONSIDERED

WITH REFERENCE TO THE QUESTION OF

A PRESBYTERIAN LITURGY.

BY

CHARLES W. SHIELDS,

PASTOR OF THE SECOND PRESBYTERIAN CHURCH, PHILADELPHIA.

PHILADELPHIA:

WILLIAM S. & ALFRED MARTIEN,

606 CHESTNUT STREET.

1863.

CONTENTS.

—◦—

NOTE.

THE following pages contain a series of articles lately contributed to the *Presbyterian*. It is hoped that their collection in this form, for continuous reading, may add to any interest occasioned by them, and shed some light upon the difficult, but vital question of which they treat.

DIRECTORY FOR PUBLIC WORSHIP,

AND THE

BOOK OF COMMON PRAYER.

————◆◆◆————

ARTICLE I.

THE ORIGIN OF THE WESTMINSTER DIRECTORY FOR PUBLIC WORSHIP.

Messrs. Editors:

As attention has lately been drawn, through your columns, and in several ecclesiastical bodies, to our "Directory for Public Worship," I have thought it might interest your readers briefly to review the history and uses, as well as abuses, of that formulary. But few Presbyterians in this country would seem to be aware of its origin, or rightly to appreciate its advantages as a mean between the extremes of imposed liturgies and "irregular, or extravagant effusions" in the service of God, as is abundantly shown by the general neglect into which it has fallen.

It may sometimes happen that Churches will have so far departed, in the progress of events, from their own early standards and usages, that the work of restoration must incur somewhat of the suspicion belonging to that of innovation; and if any of the suggestions which are to follow, should, on first thought, seem so strange as to be questionable, I trust it will be found that at least they are not mere individual conceits, or new-fangled devices.

There is also the risk of a certain odium and cheap ridicule, attending any attempts at more systematic and edifying worship, to meet which, all calm, rational argument is powerless. Without hoping to forestall the charge of being a "formalist," "liturgist," or "half Episcopalian," the writer is only anxious

2

to premise and insist upon his full right to the signature affixed to these articles.*

In reference, however, to any who are seriously interested in the subject, it is but right to say, that the views which will be advocated are believed to be scriptural, reasonable, and just; that they have not been hastily formed, but are the result of some study and experience; and that they are not meant to be here advanced without due caution and deference. It would be too much to expect a ready assent to them on the part of those who have not passed through some similar course of reflection; but it is hoped they will at least be received in the spirit in which they are offered.

No more will be attempted in this article than a glance at the history immediately preceding the establishment of the Directory. In the Scotch editions of the Confession of Faith, the document has this title—"The Directory for the Public Worship of God, agreed upon by the Assembly of Divines at Westminster, with the assistance of Commissioners from the Church of Scotland, as a part of the Covenanted uniformity in religion betwixt the Churches of Christ in the kingdoms of Scotland, England, and Ireland." But, as first adopted, and by law established, it was entitled, "A Directory for the Public Worship of God, throughout the three kingdoms of England, Scotland, and Ireland; together with an ordinance of Parliament for the taking away of the Book of Common Prayer, and the Establishing and Observing of this present Directory throughout the kingdom of England and Dominion of Wales." These titles, viewed in connection with several previous events, will afford a sufficient clue to its origin.

While the Church of Scotland differed from the Church of England in having been reformed from Popery by presbyters rather than by prelates, it agreed with it, and with all the Reformed Churches, in adhering both to the principle and to the use of a liturgy. The "Book of Common Prayer" itself, was, at one time, in use in many Presbyterian parishes;† and the "Book of Common Order," at length adopted by the

---

* "A True Presbyterian."

† Collier's Ecclesiastical History, vi. 580, vii. 388. Peterkin's Records of the Kirk of Scotland, p. iv.

General Assembly, had much in common with the Prayer-book, as will appear on comparing them. And even the first proposals to introduce the English liturgy into Scotland, were so favorably entertained by the General Assembly, that under its sanction a Prayer-book, substantially agreeing with that of the Church of England, was prepared, though never actually used.*

What might have been the result, had these measures been pursued with moderation and caution by the succeeding king, it were now simply curious to inquire. But the rise of the High Church party in England, under Laud, (the Pusey of that day,) the revival of many papistical ceremonies in the Church service, and the wild attempt of King Charles I. to impose them by force of arms upon the people of Scotland, soon dashed all hopes of uniformity or conformity in worship between the two kingdoms on the basis of any existing liturgy. It was enough to rouse the Scotch to a frenzy, that the book sent to them was a foreign production, and had not been regularly passed upon by their own Church courts, even if on examination it had been found free from errors and superstitions. The first attempt to use it in divine service at Edinburgh, was frustrated by a popular outbreak. "Fiery Presbyterians, most of them armed with good broadswords, thronged into the city;" and all ranks and orders, throughout England as well as Scotland, with a contagious enthusiasm, banded themselves together to resist the invasion, and defend the Reformed religion against the fresh inroad of the old hierarchy. To make this compact more binding and impressive, it was preceded by a public fast, and attended with the religious solemnity of an oath; the whole assembly—parliament, divines, and people, rising at the close of the service, and, with uplifted hands, uniting in a "Solemn League and Covenant,"† of which the following was the first article:

---

* Collier, vii. 388; Cook's History of Church of Scotland, Vol II. p. 336; Calderwood's True History of the Church of Scotland, pp. 5, 663, 715–17.

† "The Solemn League and Covenant, for Reformation and Defence of Religion, the honor and happiness of the King, and the peace and safety of the three kingdoms of *Scotland, England*, and *Ireland*, agreed upon by Commissioners from the Parliament and Assembly of Divines in England, with Commissioners of the Convention of Estates and General Assembly in Scotland;

"We noblemen, barons, knights, gentlemen, citizens, burgesses, ministers of the gospel, and commons of all sorts, in the kingdoms of Scotland, England, and Ireland, by the providence of God, living under one king, and being of one reformed religion, having before our eyes the glory of God, and the advancement of the kingdom of our Lord and Saviour Jesus Christ, the honor and happiness of the king's majesty and his posterity, and the true public liberty, and peace of the kingdoms, wherein every one's private condition is included; and calling to mind the treacherous and bloody plots, conspiracies, attempts and practices of the enemies of God against the true religion and professors thereof in all places, especially in these three kingdoms, ever since the reformation of religion; and how much their rage, power, and presumption are of late, and at this time, increased and exercised, whereof the deplorable state of the Church and kingdom of *Ireland*, the distressed estate of the Church and kingdom of *England*, and the dangerous estate of the Church and kingdom of *Scotland*, are present and public testimonies. We have now at last (after other means of supplication, remonstrance, protestation, and sufferings,) for the preservation of ourselves and our religion from utter ruin and destruction, according to the commendable practice of these kingdoms in former times, and the example of God's people in other nations; after mature deliberation, resolved and determined to enter into a mutual and solemn league and covenant, wherein we all subscribe, and each one of us for himself, with our hands lifted up to the Most High God, do swear,

"I. That we shall sincerely, really, and constantly, through the grace of God, endeavor, in our several places and callings, the preservation of the reformed religion in the Church of Scotland, in doctrine, worship, discipline, and government, against our common enemies; the reformation of religion in the kingdoms of England and Ireland, in doctrine, worship, discipline, and government, according to the word of God, and the example of the best Reformed Churches; and shall endeavor to bring the churches of God in the three kingdoms to the nearest conjunction and uniformity in religion, Confession of Faith, Form of Church Government, Directory for Worship, and Catechising; that we, and our people after us, may, as brethren, live in faith and love."

It was thus that the Scotch Covenanters, being now in league with the English Puritans, defeated the Prelatical party in the field, and obtained in Parliament the convocation at Westminster of that famous assembly of divines to which we owe our Directory.

---

approved by the General Assembly of the Church of *Scotland*, and by both Houses of Parliament and Assembly of Divines in *England*, and taken and subscribed by them, *Anno* 1643; and thereafter by the said authority, taken and subscribed by all ranks in *Scotland* and *England* the same year; and ratified by act of Parliament of *Scotland*, *Anno* 1644. And again renewed in *Scotland*, with an acknowledgment of sins, and engagement to duties, by all ranks, *Anno* 1648, and by the Parliament 1649; and taken and subscribed by King *Charles II.*, at Spey, June 23, 1650; and at Scoon, January 1, 1651."—*Confession of Faith of the Church of Scotland.*

ARTICLE II.

THE PRESBYTERIAN REVISION OF THE BOOK OF COMMON PRAYER AT THE SAVOY CONFERENCE.

THE reign of the Directory in the Church of England was short. The wave which had brought the Presbyterians into power soon overwhelmed them, and their religious reformation was hurried beyond their control into a political revolution. ' Having thrust down the Episcopalians, they were now, in their turn, thrust down by the Independents, or Congregationalists, and both Directory and Prayer-book sank from view in the confusions which followed.

Out of this anarchy, the Presbyterian clergy rose foremost in restoring order and peace, both to Church and State. In London, they issued a public protest against the murder of the king, and rebuked the excesses of the rebel army;* and in Scotland, they recalled his successor from exile, crowned him, and rallied to his standard, in opposition to Cromwell. And now the strange sight was presented, of Covenanter in arms against Puritan, both fighting and praying in the face of their own mutual and solemn league and covenant.

After a dreary period of defeat and disorder, the result was the reëstablishment of the throne and Constitution.ˑ But it by no means followed, that because the Presbyterians had thus been instrumental in restoring the monarchy, they also intended the restoration of that hierarchy which, from the first, had been the only object of their hostility.† Nor did it seem unreasonable that the Church of England, in accordance with the national sentiment, might continue substantially Presbyterian,

---

* "A Serious and Faithful Representation of the Judgments of the Ministers of the Gospel within the province of London." See Collier, Eccl. Hist. ix. p. 357.

† A Defence of our Proposals to his Majesty for Agreement in Matters of Religion." "The Petition of the Ministers to the King upon the First Draft of his Declaration." "Alterations in the Declaration proposed by the Ministers." See *Documents relating to the Settlement of Church of England in* 1662, pp. 39, 79, 98.

both in polity and liturgy.* The parliament and the aristocracy were then inclined to presbytery, as a safe mean between prelacy and independency. Leading prelates themselves had already favoured a "reduction of episcopacy," to be attained by making the diocesan bishop a sort of permanent moderator of presbytery;† and as the Directory had many of the rubrical elements of the Prayer-book, it was not impossible to combine the freedom and spirituality of the former, with the order and decorum of the latter, and thus, while securing their respective advantages, also escape their respective perils.

Accordingly, in the deputation which recalled Charles the Second to the throne, were such leading Presbyterian divines as Drs. Reynolds, Bates, Calamy, Baxter, &c., who presented an address‡ to the king, in which they said:

"We are satisfied in our judgments concerning the lawfulness of a Liturgy, or Form of Public Worship, provided that it be for the matter agreeable unto the Word of God, and fitly suited to the nature of the several ordinances and necessities of the Church; neither too tedious in the whole, nor composed of too short prayers, unmeet repetitions or responsals; nor to be dissonant from the Liturgies of other Reformed Churches; nor too rigorously imposed; nor

---

* "The Presbyterians," says Collier, an Episcopalian historian, "had several circumstances of advantage to support their hopes. Possession of the chair, the inclinations of no small numbers of the people, the countenance of great men, and the king's Declaration at Breda, gave this party no uncomfortable prospect."

"They represented," says Bancroft, "a powerful portion of the aristocracy of England; they had, besides the majority in the Commons, the exclusive possession of the House of Lords; they held command of the army, they had numerous and active adherents among the clergy; the English people favored them. Scotland, which had been so efficient in all that had thus far been done, was entirely devoted to their interests, and they hoped for a compromise with their Sovereign."

"The Presbyterians," says Neal, who was far from being their friend, "were in possession of the whole power of England; the council of State, the chief officers of the army and navy, and the governors of the chief forts and garrisons, were theirs; their clergy were in possession of both universities, and of the best livings of the kingdom." See Hodge's History of the Presbyterian Church, p. 25—27.

† "The Reduction of Episcopacy unto the form of Synodical Government," &c. See Documents relating to the Act of Conformity in 1661, and Calamy's Life of Baxter, chap. viii.

‡ "The First Address and Proposals of the Ministers." See Documents relating to the settlement of the Church of England by the Act of Uniformity, in 1662. London, 1862.

the minister so confined thereunto, but that he may also make use of those gifts for prayer and exhortation, which Christ hath given him for the service and edification of the Church."

"And inasmuch as the Book of Common Prayer hath in it many things that are justly offensive, and need amendment, hath been long discontinued, and very many, both ministers and people, persons of pious, loyal and peaceable minds, are therein greatly dissatisfied; whereupon, if it be again imposed, will inevitably follow sad divisions, and widening of the breaches which your Majesty is now endeavouring to heal; we do most humbly offer to your Majesty's wisdom, that for preventing so great evil, and for settling the Church in unity and peace, some learned, godly, and moderate divines, of both persuasions, indifferently chosen, may be employed to compile such a form as is before described, as much as may be in Scripture words: or at least to revise and effectually reform the old, together with an addition or insertion of some other varying forms in Scripture phrase, to be used at the minister's choice; of which variety and liberty there be instances in the Book of Common Prayer."

And the result of this application was "his Majesty's Declaration to all his loving subjects concerning Ecclesiastical Affairs,"* wherein, among other pledges given for a proper fusion of episcopacy with presbytery in the Church, was this one concerning the proposed revision of the Prayer-book:

"Since we find some exceptions made against several things therein, we will appoint an equal number of learned divines, of both persuasions, to review the same, and to make such alterations as shall be thought most necessary, and some additional forms, (in the Scripture phrase as near as may be,) suited unto the several parts of worship, and that it be left to the minister's choice to use one or other at his discretion."

For the assurances given in this Royal Declaration, the Presbyterian clergy of London presented an "Humble and Grateful Acknowledgment"† to the King, who, at the same time, appointed several of them his chaplains, while to others were offered high preferments, none of which, however, were accepted but the bishopric of Norwich, by Dr. Reynolds, and that only on the conditions of the Declaration.‡ And at length, in due form, a commission was issued for the promised revision to twelve Episcopalian divines, with nine coadjutors, and likewise to as many, the following named, Presbyterian divines, then incumbents of various livings:

---

* See Documents, &c., p. 63; Cardwell's History of Conferences on Prayer-book, p. 256.

† See Documents, &c., p. 101, and Reliquiæ Baxterianæ, by Sylvester, p. 284.

‡ Calamy's Life of Baxter, p. 155.

PRESBYTERIAN COMMISSIONERS AT THE SAVOY CONRERENCE, A. D. 1661.

Principals.	Coadjutors.
ANTHONY TUCKNEY, D. D., Regius Prof. of Div., Cambridge.	THOMAS HORTON, D. D., Prof. of Div. Gresh. Col., Cambridge.
JOHN CONANT, D. D., Regius Prof. of Div., Oxford.	THOMAS JACOMB, D. D., St. Martin's, London.
WILLIAM SPURSTOW, D. D., Mast. Katharine Hall, Cambridge.	WILLIAM BATES, D. D., St. Dunstan's, London.
JOHN WALLIS, D. D., Sav. Prof. of Geometry, Oxford.	WILLIAM COOPER, D. D., St. Olave, London.
THOMAS MANTON, D. D., St. Paul's, London.	Rev. JOHN RAWLINSON, Vicar of Lambeth.
EDMUND CALAMY, D. D., Perp. Cur. of Aldermanbury.	JOHN LIGHTFOOT, D. D.
Rev. RICHARD BAXTER, Minister at Kidderminster.	JOHN COLLINS, D. D., St. Stephens, Norwich.
Rev. ARTHUR JACKSON, St. Faith's, London.	BENJAMIN WOODBRIDGE, D. D., Vicar of Newbury.
Rev. THOMAS CASE, St. Mary Magdalen, London.	ROGER DRAKE, D. D., St. Peter's, London.
Rev. SAMUEL CLARKE, Perp. Cur. Bennet Fink, London.	
Rev. MATTHEW NEWCOMEN, Vicar of Dedham.	
EDWARD REYNOLDS, D. D., Bishop of Norwich.	

The discussions in this Conference were mainly in writing, (and are on record,) the Presbyterians bringing their "exceptions," and the Episcopalians their "rejoinders;" but from the first it was evident that no terms could be made with the latter, and the former withdrew on the failure of the Conference, in the hope of holding the King to his pledges, and obtaining redress in Parliament. Their renewed appeal concluded in these words:

"Finally, as your Majesty, under God, is the protection whereto your people fly, and as the same necessities still remain which drew forth your gracious Declaration, we most humbly and earnestly beseech your Majesty that the benefits of the said Declaration may be continued to your people; and, in particular, that none be punished or troubled for not using the common prayer, until it be effectually reviewed, and the additions made that are therein expressed. And humbly craving your Majesty's pardon for the tediousness of this address, we shall wait in hope that so great a calamity to your people, as would follow the loss of so many able, faithful ministers, as rigorous impositions would cast out, shall never be recorded in the history of your reign; but that these impediments of concord being forborne, your kingdoms may flourish in piety and peace."*

But in this hope they were doomed to be disappointed. In

* "Petition to the King at the close of the Conference." Documents, &c,. p. 379.

relying upon the vaunted "word of a king," they were leaning upon a broken reed; and with the duplicity of Charles, and the servility of Parliament, were thrown against them all the libellous influences in which that corrupt age abounded. The Prayer-book, with its exceptionable features unchanged, was presented to the House of Commons; and at length, by the close vote of 186 to 180, the House of Lords reluctantly assenting,* was passed that famous "Act of Uniformity," under the operation of which, on St. Bartholomew's Day, (now doubly memorable in our annals,) two thousand Presbyterian clergy, then unsurpassed in learning, loyalty, or piety, and comprising names whose praise is still in all the churches, chose rather to quit their livings, in the face of beggary and disgrace, than continue in an establishment unto which they could not conscientiously conform.† And, at the same time, by one of those astounding revolutions with which history sometimes sets all philosophy at defiance, Episcopacy was established in Scotland on the ruins of the Covenant and Directory.

---

* Knight's History of England, Book VIII., p. 801.

† "St. Bartholomew's day being come, on which the Act of Uniformity was to take place, two thousand Presbyterian ministers chose rather to quit their livings than to subscribe to the conditions of this Act. It was expected that a division would have happened amongst them, and that a great number of them would have chose rather to conform to the Church of England than to see themselves reduced to beggary. It was not, therefore, without extreme surprise that they were all seen to stand out,—not so much as one suffering himself to be tempted. As this is a considerable event of this reign, it will not be improper to inquire into the causes of this rigor against the Presbyterians, &c. Rapin's History of England, as quoted in Collier, ix. 453.

"On one and the same day, England saw the becoming spectacle of two thousand ministers of Jesus Christ embracing penury rather than stoop to dishonest compliance. From college halls and cathedral closes, from stately and from humble parsonages, endeared by the familiarity of happy and useful years; holy men led out their delicately nurtured families, not knowing whither they should go." Palfry's History of New England, Vol. II. p. 130.

"It is not this or that thing that puts us upon this dissent," said Jacomb, of St. Martin's, Ludgate, "but it is *conscience towards God*, and fear of offending Him. I censure none that differ from me, as though they displease God; but yet, as to myself, should I do thus and thus, I should certainly violate the peace of my own conscience, and offend God, which I must not do. Shall we not follow those who, through faith and patience, inherit the promises? Shall we leave the snow of Lebanon for Kedar and Meschech? No! let us commit ourselves to the care of our Heavenly Father. Arise! let us go hence!" Quoted in New Englander, Jan. 1863.

And thus it seemed that every vestige of Protestant liberty had been swept out of the three kingdoms. The event proved, however, that it was but a brief recoil, as if to collect strength for a last triumphant effort. In the year 1690, in the reign of King William, Presbytery again rose from under the heel of Prelacy, and achieved, in the Church of Scotland, that legal establishment which had before extinguished it in the Church of England. The Directory and the Prayer-book were driven farther apart than ever, and the two extremities of the island settled down into those extremes of Protestant churchmanship in which they have continued until the present day.

ARTICLE III.

THE GENERAL ASSEMBLY'S REVISION OF THE WESTMINSTER DIRECTORY FOR PUBLIC WORSHIP.

OUR historical sketch (in which we have aimed at truth and fairness) has brought to view these facts: 1st. That liturgies, or prescribed forms of public worship, were in use in the early Church of Scotland, as in all the Reformed Churches; 2d. That the Directory was, in its origin, a revolutionary protest against civil and ecclesiastical tyranny in such matters, and a concession to the principle of uniformity or conformity peculiar to established or State-religions; 3d. That it was followed by a healthy reaction—there having been at one time at least two thousand Presbyterian clergy in England who would have been willing to use even the Prayer-book itself, had it been properly reformed and amended; and 4th. That it was finally established by law in Scotland, as the alternative to a legally imposed liturgy, and as the only existing safeguard of a free and spiritual worship.

We come now to its history in our own country. It was certainly not necessary that these extremes, between which the Church was driven in the Old World, should have been repeated on a larger scale in the New, necessitated, as they mainly were, by political and sectarian controversies, which no longer trammel us on this side of the Atlantic; and it is not even probable that they would have been so repeated, had our fathers been able to free themselves from inherited prejudices, and to foresee the present diversified condition and relations of our Church. As it was, it is well known that in the General Assembly which adopted our Confession of Faith, the most learned and judicious members, such as Drs. Rogers, McWhorter, Ashbel Green, were in favour of so enlarging the liturgical element of the Directory, as to include in it not merely rules and topics, but complete forms for the minister's use, either as examples or materials of divine service; and the committee of revision actually prepared and reported such a liturgy, and advocated its adoption.* The failure of the scheme is not now to be wondered at, or indeed, regretted; especially since the spirit which prompted it so far prevailed in the counsels of the Assembly as to procure the amendment of the Directory in several particulars. We shall see, if we compare our edition of that formulary with the same as first adopted by the Westminster divines, that the *additions* we have made to it are decidedly liturgical in their tendency.

In the chapter on the "Preaching of the Word," we find added this much needed caution against the danger of degrading public worship into mere sermonizing:

"As one primary design of public ordinances is to pay social acts of homage to the *Most High God*, ministers ought to be careful not to make their sermons so long as to interfere with or exclude the more important duties of prayer and praise; but preserve a just proportion between the several parts of public worship."

In the chapter on the "Singing of Psalms" and hymns (which latter compositions† are not named in the Westminster formulary,) it is recommended to congregations "to cultivate some knowledge of the rules of music, that we may praise God in a becoming manner with our voices as well as with our

---

* Assembly's Digest, page 9. Eutaxia, or the Presbyterian Liturgies, Chap. xiii.

† The history of our present *Hymn-book* affords some instructive precedents in reference to the corresponding question of a *Prayer-book*, and shows how steadily the reaction has been going on in modern Presbyterianism from that false extreme into which it was driven in the Church of Scotland.

hearts;" and to ministers, "that more time be allowed for this excellent part of divine service than has been usual in most of our churches."

The chapter on "Public Prayer" is made more exact and methodical, the matter of such devotions being placed under several heads, as *Adorations, Thanksgivings, Confessions, Supplications, Pleadings,* and *Intercessions;* while, as to the manner, the use of forms is neither enjoined nor forbidden, as appears from this important amendment:

"We think it necessary to observe, that although we do not approve, as is well known, of confining ministers to set or fixed forms of prayer for public worship, yet it is the indispensable duty of every minister, previously to his entering on his office, to prepare and qualify himself for this part of his duty, as well as for preaching. He ought, by a thorough acquaintance with the Holy Scriptures, by reading the best writers on the subject, by meditation, and by a life of communion with God in secret, to endeavor to acquire both the spirit and the gift of prayer. Not only so, but when he is to enter on particular acts of worship, he should endeavor to compose his spirit, and to digest his thoughts for prayer, that it may be performed with dignity and propriety, as well as to the profit of those who join in it; and that he may not disgrace that important service by mean, irregular, or extravagant effusions."

The entire chapter on "Admission to Sealing Ordinances" is an addition, and thus extracts the kernel of truth from the error of Confirmation:

"Children born within the pale of the visible Church, and dedicated to God in baptism, are under the inspection and government of the Church, and are to be taught to read and repeat the Catechism, the Apostles' Creed, and the Lord's Prayer. They are to be taught to pray, to abhor sin, to fear God, and to obey the Lord Jesus Christ. And, when they come to years of discretion, if they be free from scandal, appear sober and steady, and have sufficient knowledge to discern the Lord's body, they ought to be informed it is their duty and privilege to come to the Lord's Supper."

While such significant additions as these are to be noticed, it is still to be regretted that the suggestions in reference to the reading of the Scriptures and of the Psalms should not have been more fully retained, and that the specific direction as to the use of the Lord's Prayer should have been inconsistently, (see Larger Catechism, Q. 187,) and no doubt inadvertently, omitted.

The Directory, as thus amended at its adoption, has remained, without material alteration, our authorized guide in public worship; but the spirit which ruled in those amendments has continued in various ways to express itself. The insertion of that form in our hymn books, designed for use in divine service; the issue by our Board of such manuals as "Miller on Public Prayer," the "Sailor's Companion; or, Book of Public and Private Devotions for Seamen," and the publication of such works as "Eutaxia, or the Presbyterian Liturgies," and ".A Book of Public Prayer, Compiled from the Authorized Formularies of the Presbyterian Church," are marks of a growing opinion in this matter; to which may be added the more practical experiment of the "St. Peter's Church," at Rochester.

Even in the mother Church of Scotland, on the very battle-ground of the Directory, the Moderator of the last General Assembly, in his opening sermon,* has recommended and ably advocated a more liturgical mode of worship, as essential to the preservation and extension of the Church in some communities. And if we choose to look around us, we shall see on every side sister Churches and denominations, occupied with the problem of a liturgy that shall retain all that is valuable in the Church

---

* He explains that there are many who-"are dissatisfied, not with our doctrine, but with our external forms of worship. The complaint is, that our services are bald and cold; that they are ill-fitted to evoke the feelings and emotions which become worshippers; that we come together rather as an audience to hear a lecturer or teacher, than to pour forth our confessions, and desires, and prayers for mercy and forgiveness through the blood of Christ; that when prayer is made, it is rather that of presiding ministers than of the assembled people; that they are wholly at the discretion of one man, however mediocre may be his gifts; that this is in no reasonable sense common prayer, for that they often toil after him in vain; that through our present system they are made passive and silent, rather than living worshippers, and are not called to confess within the sanctuary the Lord Jesus with the mouth, though it be written, 'With the heart man believeth unto righteousness; and with the mouth confession is made unto salvation.' . . . . . The regulation of these different matters, if there is truth in ecclesiastical history, was, at one period at least, left to congregations and their pastors and rulers; and to them it is humbly submitted, this Church might commit such power with greater security than any other, inasmuch as if any attempt was made to return to the forms and usages of a better age, against the mind of a major part of the congregation, or even to the offending of the honest prepossessions of a considerable portion of it, we have, through the subordination of our judicatories, ample means of granting redress."

He adds, "Many clergymen and members of the Church of Scotland, not the least in name, acquirements, and worth, have frequently discussed the matter with me, and have arrived at the same conclusion."

of the past, and yet be adapted to the Church of the present and the future.

But the general inference we would now draw from the facts before us, is, that there has always been, throughout our history, what may be called a liturgical type or phase of Presbyterianism, and that its advocates are of unimpeachable orthodoxy and piety; being so attached to our Directory as the only safe universal guide for the whole Church, that they "do not approve of confining" pastors or congregations to liturgies, and yet maintaining a voluntary and judicious use of them, in cases where it is plainly needed and desired, to be not only consistent with our standards, but part of that liberty wherewith Christ hath made his people free. And if it be asked why so little practical success has hitherto sanctioned their views, we need only mention two reasons as sufficient to account for past failures.

One fatal mistake has been that of attempting to *compose*, rather than simply to *compile*, a liturgy. The Presbyterian Commissioners in the Savoy Conference, by offering the effusion of one mind, Baxter's "Reformed Liturgy," as a fit addition to the Prayer-book, were betrayed into an error, which was most adroitly turned against them by their adversaries; and our first Assembly's Committee of Revision were on the same path, when they recommended to the whole Church, though only as a sample, a new devotional production of their own, ignoring even the hallowed formularies of Calvin and Knox. Scarcely less questionable is our Church pride and sensitiveness sometimes shown in reference to the Prayer-book, as if that excellent compilation, so largely referable to Presbyterian sources and sanctions, were an exclusively Episcopalian production, or as if it were needful to repudiate the common treasury of Christian devotion from which much of it was taken. If we intend to act upon this principle in our public worship, we must winnow out of our hymn-book its Roman Catholic, Episcopalian, and Methodist hymns, and restrict ourselves to Presbyterian poems, set to Presbyterian airs; and the reformation will not be complete until we have a Committee on "Ecclesiology," (in the pretty sense of the word,) to devise for us a church architecture, less heathen or more Protestant than the

Greek or Gothic temples in which some of our congregations are content to worship. The truth is, that, strictly speaking, a liturgy, like a creed or confession, cannot be the product of any one mind or age, or even sect of the Church; and it is no wonder that good sense and good taste have always combined with true piety in eschewing forms of worship, whether prescribed or extemporaneous, which are full of individual conceits and capricious novelties.

But the other, and not less serious, mistake which has been made, is that of hoping to impose, or in any way introduce a liturgy throughout the entire Church, without regard to its diversified condition. We have seen that our whole history is a protest against the interference of the civil power in such matters; many things in the Prayer-book which were simply indfferent, or even laudable, having been resisted to the utmost, when by law enjoined as terms of communion; and the same instinct of liberty rises against any abuse of even Church power in the details of public worship. The genius of presbytery, the world over, cannot endure any thing more stringent than a Directory, or system of general rules and suggestions; and to picture her vast communion, ministers and congregations, servilely drilled through a course of changing vestments, intonations, and demeanors, would be the wildest of fancies. It may be questioned, indeed, whether so simple a thing as an ecclesiastical recommendation, though it were in favor of the best liturgy that could be framed, would be, if warrantable, on any account desirable. Our Church, as a Church, might find in such appliances a hindrance to her own growth, efficiency, and spirituality; as is shown by the fact, that the denomination which adheres to an imposed liturgy cannot take it effectively outside of the cities, into the country, or to the frontiers. Moreover, in a land so vast and varied as ours, any thing like strict uniformity of worship is, in the nature of things, unattainable. It is unreasonable that a congregation in St. Louis or New York should have all its appliances of devotion exactly like those of a congregation in the interior of Pennsylvania, or of Kansas, and such a rigid correspondence does not, in fact, exist throughout our bounds. The Church has, therefore, wisely foreborne either to enjoin or to forbid choirs, organs, particular styles of architecture and furniture, or a stated order and form of the several parts of public worship; and it may be safely assumed that all parties would unite in deprecating any ecclesiastical action in reference to such questions, as not only unnecessary, but an invasion of that constitutional liberty in things indifferent, which we prize as second only to our uniformity in things essential.

In several remaining articles we propose to discuss the existing abuses of our Directory, or the evils which have arisen under it, and the available remedies and improvements.

ARTICLE IV.

MINISTERIAL NEGLECTS, AND THEIR REMEDIES UNDER THE DIRECTORY.

IN public worship, the two human parties are the minister and the congregation—the former leading in the service, and the latter accompanying him with the heart, or in some parts, with the voice also; and, for the guidance of these two parties, the Directory gives certain general rules and suggestions. Let us consider, in this article, the ministerial requisites of edifying worship; and we would do this in no censorious or critical spirit, but only out of love to that Church which is the mother of us all, and from a conviction that the defects in our present practice are already generally admitted and regretted, and all the more readily, because they are not past remedy. The writer, indeed, is simply confessing for himself, as well as for others.

And let it be candidly asked, at the outset, if our ministry have not, as a body, widely departed from the direction that "one primary design of public ordinances is to pay social acts of homage to the *Most High God;*" and if, in yielding to the popular taste for able and eloquent sermons, they are not neglecting the prescribed general and special preparation "for this part of their duty as well as for preaching?" No true

Presbyterian, indeed, would wish to see the pulpit thrust aside in our worship. It is the glory of Protestant, as it was of primitive Christianity; and our Church, in so carefully furnishing herself with a race of educated preachers and scholars, has acquired a hold upon the intellectual classes, as distinguished from the merely fashionable, or the merely vulgar, which makes her the bulwark of all conservatism throughout the land. But while we have thus signally escaped the evil which existed when, according to the Westminster divines,* "the reading of common prayer was made no better than an idol by many ignorant and superstitious people, who, pleasing themselves in their presence at that service, and their lip-labour in bearing a part in it, have thereby hardened themselves in their ignorance and carelessness of true knowledge and saving piety," may we not meanwhile have lapsed towards the opposite error, of making no better than an idol the reading of a sermon, by so allowing it to "exclude or interfere with the more important duties of prayer and praise," that they are degraded into a mere hasty prelude of the preacher, or "disgraced with mean, irregular, or extravagant effusions."

Some eminent exceptions, indeed, there are to this general neglect; but it cannot be denied that in too many cases there is neither "a just proportion between the several parts of public worship," nor any evidence of the required carefulness that they "may be performed with dignity and propriety, as well as to the profit of those who join in them." The matter, form, and arrangement of them have been left to chance or impulse. The psalms, hymns, and Scripture readings, or lessons, are selected at random, or upon no obvious principle; and the prayers are long and rambling effusions of what happens to come uppermost in the mind. All is vague, crude, and unedifying; and the congregation, sympathizing with the preacher, are glad to despatch their devotions and come to the sermon, where they can have something more orderly and intelligible.

It is, indeed, often urged, in extenuation of these evils, that worshippers are, or ought to be, in a less critical mood during the devotional than the more didactic part of the service, and

---

* Preface to the Westminster Directory.

3

certain texts are quoted in favor of the minister's literally taking no thought what shall be said, and relying upon the Holy Spirit absolutely for good utterance, as well as right feeling. It would be easy to parry such texts, and to quote counter-texts;—"God is not the author of confusion in the churches of his saints;" "I will pray with the Spirit, and I will pray with the understanding also;" "Let all things be done decently and in order;" or to cite that methodical form of devotion, combining both directory and liturgy, which our Lord taught his disciples. But we admit the general principle asserted, while we still insist upon its proper limitations. The most acceptable and edifying public worship is, unquestionably, that in which the minister's form and the people's feeling are directly prompted by the Holy Ghost; and yet what shall be said of that in which the form does not fully express the feeling, but in many ways positively thwarts or destroys it—in which there is no well-ordered system of hymns, psalms, lessons, and prayers, by which to excite, sustain, and guide devotion; and in which the worshipper is either driven from public into private prayer, or rendered the worst of formalists? The late Dr. Miller, in his work upon this subject,* has enumerated many, but by no means all, of the defective forms or modes of public prayer, such as the *repetitious*, the *tedious*, the *irreverent*, the *incoherent*, the *unseasonable*, the *political*, the *complimentary*, the *didactic*, the *rhetorical*, the *sarcastic*, &c. We ask, in all Christian candor, if it is not a gross abuse of the doctrine of spiritual gifts and influences, to rank such effusions as utterances of the Holy Ghost, or to impose them upon a worshipping assembly as *their* prayers? They are not theirs, and cannot be made theirs, any further than they actually express the desires of their hearts, and are, on their part, intelligently and devoutly offered up unto God.

And this great and growing neglect is already telling injuriously upon our whole system. We believe we only utter a common sentiment, when we say that, on the one hand, it has increased the taste for a style of "sensational" preaching which but few ministers can acquire or sustain ; and, on the

---

* Miller on Public Prayer, Chap. iv.

other hand, has rendered all public prayer and praise a mere
foil to the sermon. The pulpit has become the rival of the
rostrum, and mere intellectual entertainment substituted for
devout communion with God. The people take refuge from
the service in the discourse, and the discourse is elaborated at
the expense of the service. Whereas, the need of careful preparation for the one only exceeds that for the other by as much
as what is offered in the form of prayer or praise to God, is
more momentous than what is addressed in the form of mere
argument or appeal to man.

Now, the obvious remedy for these evils is to have some plan
or method of preparing and conducting the several parts of
public worship, by means of which the whole service shall be
made at least coherent and intelligible. With most ministers
the only plan would seem to be to adapt the lessons, hymns,
and prayers mainly to the sermon. But, while this may be
convenient, it can scarcely be called reasonable; for, unless his
subject has been before announced, or the occasion itself is
suggestive, the congregation are left to grope after him, vaguely
guessing his meaning, or else to worship without any intelligent
sympathy with him, or with one another. Leaving this principle to be adopted when circumstances require it, a better method, we suggest, would be ordinarily to frame the services
before the discourse entirely independent of it, or at least to
have some obvious system in which the sermon shall follow as
part of the worship, and not the worship precede as a mere
vague prologue to the sermon. The reason for this is, that
there are certain "social acts of homage," which every congregation, on ordinary occasions, ought to offer, whatever may be
the particular theme the preacher has chosen. Besides his
special instruction, there are acts of confession, supplication,
intercession, thanksgiving, praise, and hearing of God's word,
which must be suited to the various classes, states, and charac-
ters of a mixed assembly, and without which their service cannot be called public worship. And to say that every minister
can properly express and conduct these varied devotions without any plan or forethought, is to say what every minister
knows to be simply impossible. It is for the want of such plan
and forethought that large portions of the Scriptures are never

read in our churches; that there is scarcely ever a complete
service in which no part is slighted or exaggerated, and no
class of worshippers neglected, and that in general the ministrations of each pastor are of necessity so impressed with his
own individuality, that the people neither receive from God his
whole Word, nor can publicly offer to God their whole heart.
And though we would not have the ministry, as a body, come
under the bondage of an inflexible system, yet we see no reason
why any minister might not for himself so systematize the ordinary church service as to secure at once his own convenience
and profit, and the edification of his fellow-worshippers. The
leading features of such a system may be briefly indicated as
follows:

1. He might arrange a yearly course of Scripture lessons for
the instruction of the people in the entire word of God, by
reading in every service from both Testaments (according to
the suggestion of the original Directory,) not necessarily whole
chapters, (which divisions are not inspired, and are often too
lengthy for a single reading,) but brief portions, selected in the
order of the sacred books themselves, or upon some other scriptural and rational principle. As Christ is the end and sum of
both dispensations, there could be no more effective mode of
unfolding the whole divine revelation than that of converging,
Sabbath after Sabbath, the blended light of *history* and *prophecy*,
of *gospel* and *epistle*, upon the leading events of his life, and the
main features of his doctrine. And these lessons might be
separated or followed by a *prayer* or *hymn* in keeping with
them, or suited to give devotional expression to them. Such
an arrangement, besides imparting variety and unity to the
service, would also afford that much-needed relief and help, a
stated supply of themes for the sermon.

2. He might adhere to some simple method in the stated
public prayers, by at least keeping each class of them distinct
and proportionate, so that neither the *confessions*, nor *supplications*, nor *intercessions*, nor *thanksgivings* of the congregation
should be omitted, nor "the whole rendered too short or too
tedious." The Directory further recommends, besides the cultivation of personal piety, pre-arrangement and pre-meditation
as to the matter of such devotions; but whether as to the form

of them, there should be any thing like composition or compilation from the Scriptures, and the best models, is not decided, and cannot be, by any general rule. "Let every man be fully persuaded in his own mind." It is certain, that the public prayers of some of the holiest and most gifted ministers, such as Drs. Green and Chalmers, were often as carefully prepared as their sermons; and it is equally certain, that the ministrations of other eminent preachers would have been greatly improved by such preparation. Those who most oppose it, are generally those who most need it. There is much ignorant prejudice in reference to this grave matter. Because the warm, unstudied effusions of a good man, evidently in communion with God, and himself as remarkable for prudence as for piety, are confessedly better than the most sincere recitation, and infinitely better than the mere formal reading of prayers, we absurdly elevate the rare exception into a rule. But there is no practical evidence in our ministry to support the specious pretension; and until the preacher has given proof of an apostolic gift of utterance, it is surely questionable whether he ought to leave his follow-worshippers wholly at the mercy of his moods and caprices.

3. He might arrange the several parts of worship in some natural order or succession, by which the worshipper should be conducted from the simple to the more difficult and intimate stages of devotion; beginning with an Invocation, or act of Humiliation and Confession, and thence proceeding to the Reading of the Law and the Gospel, with Confession of Faith, through the Supplications and Intercessions, to the crowning acts of Thanksgiving and Praise. And sometimes might be used with profit those excellent summaries of these several parts of public service, the *Commandments*, the *Beatitudes*, the *Apostles' Creed*, the *Lord's Prayer*, and that well-digested series of petitions contained in the reformed *Litany*, the whole being preceded by one of the reformed *Confessions*.

4. He might both have and use a form in those ceremonial offices, for which the Directory provides only general rules, but which cannot, in the nature of the case, be wholly extemporized —such as the "Administration of Baptism," "Administration of the Lord's Supper," "Admission of Persons to Sealing

Ordinances," "Solemnization of Marriage," "Burial of the Dead," &c. It is matter of general complaint, if not loud, yet deep, that these solemn occasions are so often marred by crude and random effusions. If only a few well-chosen sentences of Scripture were pronounced at such times, it would be far better than the mere desultory harangues to which intelligent and devout assemblies are sometimes subjected.

But to sum up all in one word, the minister might have an exemplified Directory or Liturgy of his own, such as was common in all the early and some of the modern Presbyterian churches. If the only objection would be, the labour of composing or compiling it, we hope yet to show that this is an objection which can easily be avoided.

ARTICLE V.

CONGREGATIONAL NEGLECTS AND THEIR REMEDIES UNDER THE DIRECTORY.

WHATEVER may be the abuses and evils in the ministerial department of our public worship, we believe them to be fully equalled by those which prevail in that of the congregation; and because the latter are the parties primarily interested, their peculiar errors, as well as rights and duties, should be all the more freely canvassed. It would, indeed, be much pleasanter to picture our whole theory, realized both in a ministry endowed with apostolic gifts, and in assemblies rapt in pentecostal fervors; but let it be remembered that the very first step towards amendment, is to deal honestly with the facts as we find them.

And we, therefore, affirm it to be as undeniable as it is lamentable, that in many of our congregations a growing suppression has been taking the place of all proper expression of devotional feeling. Judging by appearances, in some cases, the great mass would seem no longer to go to church to worship God, so much as to hear choirs and sermons. They sit between the pulpit and the organ, in mute compliance, while their prayers and praises are performed by proxy. With all our boasted Protestantism, we have in the heart of our communion the essence of the Roman ritual, a *vicarious service*, of which the people are but auditors, and in which, sometimes, they can no more individually participate than if priest and choir were praying and singing for them in a separate performance.

Some signal exceptions, indeed, there may be to this general decline of congregational worship; but the mournful fact is conspicuous, that our assemblies, as a class, neither "praise God in a becoming manner, with their voices, as well as with their hearts," nor intelligently unite in "offering up their desires to God for things agreeable to his will." Those solemn functions have been delegated to the choir and the preacher, in whose hands they have become respectively mere artistic performances, and individual rhapsodies. In many cases the people do not, simply because they cannot, pray or sing; and the words, "Let us pray," or "Let us sing," are but dead formulas—hints of a duty, echoes of a reality.

It is sometimes urged, in extenuation of these abuses, that the several parts of divine service ought to be thus committed to qualified proxies, in order that by the free exercise of their superior gifts, under the influence of the Holy Ghost, the body of worshippers shall be edified; and the example of the primitive Christian assemblies is cited in illustration. We need not deny the general doctrine, while we insist that it should at least be carefully and consistently applied. That is unquestionably the most edifying form of public worship, in which those most gifted in prayer and praise shall lead, while the rest of the assembly accompany or follow them; but even the inspired prophets and many-tongued psalmists, in the early Church, were admonished by the apostle to be intelligible, as well as fervent, and on no pretence to intrude mere private rhapsody into public worship. So likewise now, the minister may "pray with the Spirit;" but except he "pray with the understanding also," and "utter by the tongue words easy to be understood, how shall it be known what is spoken, for he shall speak into the air?" And the minstrels may "sing with

the Spirit;" but except they "sing with the understanding
also," and "give a distinction in the sounds, how shall it be
known what is piped or harped?" If it be granted that each
"edifieth himself," yet it cannot be said that "the church is
edified;" and when it is evident that neither party is edified,
but that the public praises are a mere display of soprano, con-
tralto, tenor, and bass, by an invisible quartette, and the public
prayers a mere exposure of the preacher's own personal feelings, and even conceits, prejudices, and errors, "how shall he
that occupieth the room of the unlearned (layman or private
person) say Amen?". We sometimes hear the services criti-
cised, not less freely than the sermon, as "interesting," "impressive," "beautiful," "eloquent," or as the reverse of these.
In the name of the Apostle, we ask if this was what he meant
by "excelling in spiritual gifts, to the edifying of the church,"
or if such performances themselves can, in any proper sense,
be regarded as "social acts of homage to the Most High God."

And the natural effect of this vicarious system has been, not
only to rob the people of their prayers and praises, but to
destroy all wholesome relish on their part for more congregational worship, if not, in some cases, to foster a depraved taste
for the *impressive*, rather than the *expressive* forms of religious
service. How could this be otherwise? The worshipper, from
being a passive auditor, easily becomes a mere critic of the
whole performance, and craves only what shall pleasantly affect
his ear or his imagination, or readily fall in with his taste and
prejudices. According as the choir do their part, well or ill,
he approves or disapproves. If he is sometimes "prayed into
a good mood" by the preacher, he is at other times "prayed
out of it." And thus he becomes more regardful of the human
agents in worship, than of the Divine majesty and presence,
and loses that sense of individual responsibility, which would be
sustained and kept awake, were he expressing his own feeling
by actually taking part, audibly and intelligently, with others
in common acts of devotion.

Now, it must be admitted that these are, to some extent,
necessary evils, not absolutely peculiar to our system of worship; and that the most direct and effective remedy for them
is to be sought in the cultivation of an earnest and spiritual

piety, on the part of both ministers and people. It is, indeed, most true, that did both parties habitually live near to God, and come together in the church full of the Holy Ghost, our worshipping assemblies would be shaken as with a mighty wind of holy fervor, and pray and sing as with tongues of flame; and in times of revival, we are brought to some faint appreciation of this lost ideal. But it is sheer folly, in the face of such facts as have been detailed, to act upon a theory fit only for prophets and psalmists, and even by them only too soon and sadly perverted; and if we would escape that spasmodic type of piety, which at once necessitates and abuses revivals of religion, we must not, in ordinary times at least, disdain the means of normal, healthy growth and culture.

We would, therefore, advocate the use of any right expedients which can be devised for bringing the congregation into more direct sympathy and outward union with the minister, and with one another, in their common devotions. Nothing which can further such important ends is too insignificant to be considered. In social services, such a trifle as gathering together a thin, scattered assembly, into a compact body, will free them from the sense of formality and coldness that would otherwise prevail; and in more public services, a similar benefit might be attained by bringing the minister down from his stilted pulpit, and the choir out of their distant loft, and more visibly and audibly associating them with the mass of their fellow-worshippers. But without dwelling upon such details, we will limit ourselves to one or two general suggestions, which we believe to be legitimate and practical.

1. It would greatly promote congregational devotion, or true public worship, to restore to the whole assembly their peculiar privilege and bounden duty of "praising God by singing psalms or hymns, publicly in the church." There is that in the very act of such vocal utterance which is fitted to express and nourish holy feeling; and choirs, organs, choristers, or precentors, only succeed in their vocation in so far as they develope it from the mass of worshippers. It is accordingly recommended in the Directory, "that we cultivate some knowledge of the rules of music," and that "the whole congregation should be furnished with books, and ought to join in this

part of worship;" for both of which duties excellent provision has been made in our Psalmodist and Hymn Book. It may be questioned however, whether either Rouse's or Watts' version of the Psalms is to be preferred, either on the score of poetry, or of music, or of devotion, to the literal version chanted by the choir and people. The responsive reading of the Psalter, though only confusing, and anything but solemn to one not taking part in it, has, however, the recommendation that it engages the attention, and helps the devotion of every worshipper; since all may read, though all cannot sing.

2. It would also be a great improvement, if the congregation could join more intelligently in the public prayers, as well as praises, by being no less positively associated with the minister than with the chorister. We cannot see any such intrinsic difference between the two services as to demand the diverse practice respecting them. If it is indispensable, in the nature of the case, to extemporize the prayers, why not also to improvise the hymns? or if an assembly may devoutly use forms of praise, may they not as devoutly use forms of prayer. The mere intellectual effort of composing or following extemporaneous productions, in the solemn act of public devotion, is very often unfavourable to simple, earnest feeling. The listener becomes entangled with the speaker in sentence-making, or is repelled by expressions or sentiments which, to say the least, he cannot readily adopt and offer up as his own. But, could both parties agree, as touching what things they will ask, and unite together in the use of the same words, there would certainly be less to hinder or distract their common act of worship.

Whether audible responses ought also to be added, as a further help to congregational devotion, is a question of usage and taste, rather than of principle. It cannot be denied, that in the ancient Jewish and early Christian assemblies, the "private person," as the phrase, "he that occupieth the room of the unlearned" might be properly rendered, was wont literally to "say Amen." And when we hear the fervid ejaculations of Methodists on the one side, and the methodical responses of Episcopalians on the other, we cannot affirm the custom to be in itself either undevout or indecorous. Nor can it be proved to be wholly un-presbyterian. In our early liturgies, says the author of "Eutaxia," "the prayers, by constant use made familiar to the people, were to be followed silently, or in subdued tones." The minister invited the people to make the Confession of Sins, "following in heart these words," or "sincerely saying." And perhaps this mental accompaniment and silent Amen are to be preferred, on the whole, either to the noisy outcries or the confused murmuring of our neighbors. The main thing is, that the attention and devotion be easily sustained, and whether the voice join or respond, is immaterial, if only the minister's form, (for some form every minister does and must have,) be so *simple, suitable,* and *well-known,* that each worshipper can follow it without intellectual fatigue or confusion, and with a fully assenting mind.

Besides the *Amen* in ancient worship was used the *Selah,* or pause for silent devotion, which, though also designed as a "rest" in the musical performance of praise, might equally well, in accordance with modern usage, be employed for prayer. As there are times or moods in which the minister will be prompted to fresh, unpremeditated utterances, for which no formulary can make due provision, so there may be occasions, in solemn assemblies, especially in time of communion at the Lord's table, when intervals of silence will conduce far more than speech to true spiritual worship. Let us not disdain devotional helps, from whatever source they may be taken, but remember that no usage becomes widely prevalent which is not founded in some legitimate want of human nature, whether it be the speechless Quaker meeting, or the occasional revival, or the random Amen and Hallelujah of the Methodist, or the formal Litany and Collects of the Episcopalian. It is rather the dictate of wisdom to cull out the good from the evil, and, if possible, avoid the abuses and extremes of a partial system, by combining occasional free prayer of the minister, and silent prayer of the worshipper, with stated prayers for the whole congregation.

3. It would complete the ideal we are framing, if the congregation, besides thus participating both in the prayers and in the praises, could also intelligently follow the minister through his scheme of lessons, psalms, and hymns for each Sunday of the yearly course, by means of a service-book or manual, com-

panion to our Directory and Hymn-book. Whatever might be
the advantage to the pastor of such a scheme, that to the people would be ten-fold greater, as it would bring them into perfect sympathy with him, and render their public worship what
it ought to be—a systematic instruction in the whole letter of
Scripture, together with an intelligent offering up unto God of
those ordinary prayers and praises which are proper to every
Christian assembly.

In a word, supposing such a system of divine service to have
been composed or compiled, in any case where the parties
should be mutually so disposed, the minister and congregation
might agree, under the general rules of our Directory, (as, indeed, has already been done in at least one instance,*) to conduct their public devotions by the aid of a liturgy. There are,
we are aware, grave prejudices and objections to this, which
ought to be duly weighed; and we therefore propose to consider
them in another article.

ARTICLE VI.

THE CONSISTENCY OF A FREE LITURGY WITH THE DIRECTORY.

WE are met on the threshold of the question as to liturgies,
by a prejudice and a misconception, neither of which we believe to be scriptural, reasonable, or truly Presbyterian.

Of the prejudice, which does undoubtedly prevail, let it be
said, in the first place, that it is by no means universal, but
has taken root most widely and deeply in the Scotch and
Scotch-Irish portions of our Church. We do not wish to be
misunderstood. It is one of the chief excellencies of our system, whereby its true catholicity is approved, that it is of no
mere national or local origin, and cannot be absorbed in any
single ecclesiastical organization, such as the Church of Rome,
or the Church of England, or the Church of Scotland; but
flourishes in all lands, in connection with all races, and under
all political systems. Besides the Scotch type of Presbytery,
we have the Dutch, the German, the French, and the English;

---

* See the "Church-Book of St. Peter's Church," Rochester, N. Y.

and these several elements have been so fused together in our American communion, and in almost every Presbyterian family that has been long enough in the country, that no true son of such a Church can be suspected of blaming or praising one to the disparagement or advantage of the other. While, therefore, we hold to the staunch orthodoxy of John Knox against all Papistical superstitions, and pantomimic performances in church, ancient or recent, we may now at least demur to his destructive zeal against a certain Book of Common Prayers, about which his conscience was straitened in the time of the Papal persecutions, but concerning which, even then, he could draw from his teacher, John Calvin, no harsher sentence than that it contained *multas tolerabiles ineptias* (many endurable trifles); and although, as all the world knows, Presbytery got the better of Prelacy at Marston-Moor and Naseby, and was finally only cheated out of the Church of England by a majority of a few votes,* yet we may begin to query whether, when the Assembly's divines came to a word-fight with his Majesty's High-Church chaplains, and so ably argued that presbyters, and not bishops, were true successors of the Apostles, we were not, however, somewhat worsted on the liturgical question; and whether, upon the whole, such learned and godly Presbyterians as Thomas Manton, Edmund Calamy, William Bates, Richard Baxter, did not show better logic and wisdom in afterwards striving to purge out the *tolerabiles ineptias*, than to throw away the gold with the dross. The truth is, that throughout all these troubles, our Church was passing between the two fires of Prelacy and Independency, liturgy and conventicle—escaping unhurt, indeed, though not without marks of the flame; and to this day the motto of the mother Kirk still suits the dilemma of her American daughter—*Nec tamen consumebatur*, with the difference, that we now lean too near to the Puritan, to be in much danger of the Churchman.

But, in the second place, it could easily be shown that even our Scotch prejudice against liturgies is both unintelligent and inconsistent. The simple fact is, that the Church of Scotland, although at present non-liturgical, is not, and never has been anti-liturgical, but was driven into its negative position by "the

---

* See page 13.

unjustifiable efforts of Laud and his master to force a justly
obnoxious liturgy upon a free people;"* and as one of the ill
effects of that unhappy controversy, we inherit a morbid terror
of everything approaching to form in public worship. But the
earlier usage, even in the days of Knox, as we have seen, was
very different. "The Book of Common Order, or the Order
of the English Kirk at Geneva, whereof John Knox was Minister: approved by the famous and learned man, John Calvin;
received and used by the Reformed Kirk of Scotland, and ordinarily prefixed to the Psalms in Metre: A. D. 1600," has all
the elements of a complete liturgy, and contains, in common
with the Prayer-book, as parts of the ordinary service, a Confession of Sins, the Lord's Prayer, the Apostles' Creed, a
Prayer for the whole estate of Christ's Church, &c., besides
the marriage service nearly verbatim, the ceremony of the
ring excepted. We have seen under what pressure of Prelacy
on the one side, and dragging of Independency on the other,
we were at length forced away from both these liturgies into
the Directory. But it is surely neither wise nor consistent to
continue under the dominion of a prejudice due to such causes.
   There is, however, in connection with this prejudice, a misconception which has, no doubt, tended to strengthen and per-
petuate it, and which may even remain after it has been
exposed, or where it does not prevail. We refer to the common mistake of confounding a liturgy with an artistic ritual or
elaborate ceremonial service. The word calls up, in some
minds, the image of a Gothic building, with stained windows,
admitting "dim, religious light"—a mysterious chancel, with
altar, lecturn, and pulpit, adjusted on recondite principles—an
intoning figure in white surplice, with book in hand, and a gaily
dressed assembly manœuvering through the parade duty of
certain genuflexions, recitations, responses, bowings, &c.; and
if all this is to be dragged in the net of a liturgy, we admit
that our present labour has been in vain. What has been
described, however, in previous articles, has nothing to do with
such accessories, and would be vitiated by admixture with
them. We have advocated no particular style of church architecture and furniture, or of ministerial dress, or of congrega-

* **Eutaxia,** p. 260.

tional behaviour, and have proposed no innovations in such matters; but, leaving them where the Directory leaves them, have simply maintained that there might be, and, in some cases, there ought to be, in connection with the faithful preaching of God's word, a system of common devotions for both minister and people, whereby they could methodically become acquainted with the Holy Scriptures, and statedly, by simple spiritual acts of worship, offer up their public prayers and praises "with the spirit and with the understanding also." With the Presbyterian divines at the Savoy Conference, we have judged that "Prayer, confession, thanksgiving, reading of the Scriptures, and administration of the sacraments, in the plainest and simplest manner, were matter enough to furnish out a sufficient liturgy, though nothing either of private opinion, or of church pomp, of garments, or prescribed gestures, of imagery, of music, of matter concerning the dead, of many superfluities which creep into the Church under the name of *order* and *decency*, did interpose itself."

Such a liturgy we believe to be not only consistent with true Presbyterianism, but a legitimate development of it, which has hitherto been hindered by untoward influences, and which is already urgently needed to defend the weak point of our system, and equip it for the work of church-extension in all directions. And its judicious introduction by agreement of the two parties concerned, need not occasion any interference with the rights of those congregations which prefer a different usage, nor any more serious diversity than already, and of necessity, prevails in our practice.

Of the objections that may be raised to such a liturgy, the most plausible is, that it would tend to formalism in worship. We do not wish to slur this objection, but to sift it as thoroughly as can be, in the absence of a fair experiment, by which alone the question could be decided. It would indeed be but right to first take into account the alternative evils to which we are exposed. There may be such things as hypocrisy, cant, extravagance, and superstition, as well as formality in divine service; and when there is no fresh impulse or occasion of devotion, it will not be strange, it will simply be unavoidable, that, in the absence of a well-ordered form to excite and cherish holy feeling, there should be forced or feigned excitement.

We arc not speaking of what ought to be, but of what arc, the facts. Let us not deceive ourselves, but look at the question on all sides, and we may possibly reach the conclusion, that at times a liturgy might prove a help rather than a hindrance to true spiritual worship. When the minister's spirit is clouded and heavy, his written sermon is a great relief, and may even gradually warm him up into genuine fervor, and his whole audience with him; or if he eschew preparation and paper, and halt and trip in his utterance, large excuses can still be made for one who comes speaking to the people in the name of God; but when he turns to speak to God in the name of the people, is it perfectly reasonable that the devotions of some hundreds of worshippers should be left dependent upon the state of his digestion? The spirit may be willing, but the flesh is weak. He might, perhaps, take some old familiar words in company with them, and at least not hinder their devotion or his own; but to absolutely make new prayers for them, *ex tempore*, every Sunday, under dread of falling into a *form* of prayer—alas! is it not enough that he should make two able and eloquent sermons?

Some form there must be, in all edifying worship. Without it, we relapse towards Methodist extravagance or Quaker apathy. Some form there is in every pastor's mode of conducting worship. He glides into a service almost as stereotyped as the dreaded liturgy. It is, after all, the thing without the name; and the only question really worth considering is, whether that liturgy shall be a good one or a bad one. The advocates of a supposed impromptu service, springing up in perennial freshness, and ceaseless variety, do not seem rightly to distinguish between public and private devotion, or between ordinary and extraordinary states of religious feeling. In social meetings, especially during seasons of revival, or on marked providential occasions, the whole outward expression of worship will indeed be free and artless, and any thing like forms would be felt as an intolerable bondage; but in large assemblies, convened for stated acts of homage, there cannot but be more of system, sameness, and pre-arrangement. Nor is it easy to see what advantage would be gained by an ingenious variety, or capricious novelty, so far as that is possible in reference to the ordinary devotions of a congregation, when there might be customary forms of expressing them, which have been used and sanctioned by the learned and godly of all churches and ages; which being largely taken from the very words of Scripture, concisely express the wants, the fears, the doubts, the hopes, and the joys of all Christians; and which are marked by a simple majesty of style, a chaste fervour, tenderness, and solemnity, utterly unknown in any modern compositions. In the open, voluntary use of such helps to devotion, both parties might find a mutual relief and profit, which must be foregone so long as either the people are at the mercy of random effusions, or the minister is hampered with a surreptitious form of his own.

We may add, that the objection now under consideration is not supported by facts. Some of the most spiritually-minded men that ever lived, have used and contended for a liturgy; but formalists will be formal under any system.

Another and kindred objection is, that a liturgy would repress all originality on the part of the minister, and foster a deadly monotony in his services. The life of public worship, it is argued, consists in that vivid impression made by an earnest speaker, with heart aglow, and voice and tone spontaneously giving forth every petition as an expression of his own personal feeling. Such prayers, it is said, are more "interesting," "solemn," or "touching," than any recited form, however appropriate. We admit this personal or individual element to be a great advantage in the sermon, and even, with proper limitations, in the service. The very best preaching and praying are confessedly extemporaneous, and also the *very worst*. It depends entirely upon the person, the mood, the occasion, and the circumstances; and when all of these are not perfectly favorable, then the question presents another aspect. The Apostle's rule is, "Let all things be done to edifying;" and there may be, as we have seen, individual peculiarities or originalities in public prayer which are not edifying. Because the broken, confused utterances of some private suppliant are far better for him than any form, it does not follow that they will also be more edifying to a whole assembly, nor is it quite clear that any sentimental advantage or pathetic interest gained

4

by their exposure, is not more than balanced by the risk of a
certain vanity, embarrassment, or indelicacy, on the one side,
together with a certain admiration, regret, or pity, on the other.
Ah! it may be pardonable in us to like to hear a good sermon;
but is it worshipping God to love to hear how well a man can
pray? and do we not sometimes see the "gift of prayer" without the grace, as well as the grace without the gift?

Moreover, the objection we are considering is valid only on
the assumption, that the minister is so slavishly tied down to
rules and forms, that he cannot, when the fresh mood or new
occasion prompts him, break away from them into more spontaneous services. It would, of course, be impossible to frame
either directions or samples for every possible emergency; and
the only proper design of a liturgy is, to give edifying expression to those stated public devotions which are in their nature
fixed and invariable, while all the benefits of the most informal
worship may still be sufficiently retained in the lecture and
prayer-meetings during the week, or in the second service on
the Lord's day, as well as by blending free with stated prayer,
on all occasions, at discretion.

A far more specious scruple is, that liturgies foster an "æsthetic" form of devotion, or cultivate the taste and imagination
at the expense of the heart and conscience. Some persons, it
is asserted, are of a liturgical temperament, and by dwelling
critically upon the form in distinction from the matter or spirit
of worship, at length become so fastidious, that they cannot
worship God unless it be in good English, and with all the
little outward proprieties carefully adjusted; and this, it is
hinted, is a weakness and folly, which ought to be mortified as
one of the remainders of the old Adam.

Now, it need not be denied that there may be an excess of
even so good a thing as good taste; but, on the other hand, it
cannot be denied that the holiest things may be spoiled by so
trifling a thing as a little bad taste. And when old-fashioned
Presbyterians, or their descendants, are found worshipping in
imitation Parthenons or Westminster Abbeys, with the aid of
costly music and oratory, we ask if it is not simply a question
of good sense, and of the most ordinary piety, what shall be
the literary or intellectual character of their liturgy; and

whether, on the whole, it would not be wiser and more profitable, not to say in better taste, either to lay aside all these fine artistic surroundings, and relapse to Rouse and the precentor, two hours' sermons, and half-hour prayers, or else to find vent for the irrepressible "æsthetic" element, where it better comports with our system, in the form of a reasonable service?

No one, who thinks and observes, believes that true taste and true devotion are in their nature antagonistic, or that where they are found together, they can be rigorously driven apart. A congregation accustomed to refinement in their homes, will have it also in their church; and experience has shown, that, while a liturgy may indeed be more edifying to cultivated and intellectual Christians, than "mean, irregular, or extravagant effusions," yet it may also unite together all tastes, good, bad, and indifferent.

As to the objection, that it would cost us something of church pride and consistency, or expose us to ridicule as imitators, it is enough to say, in view of the historical facts already presented, that the sooner all parties are rid of this idea the better.

The only remaining difficulty we now think of is, the want of a suitable manual or service-book, sanctioned by sufficient Presbyterian authority to insure its orthodoxy, and encourage its use. We believe this objection to be the most serious that can be raised; but by no means insuperable, as we hope may appear in our next and last article.

ARTICLE VII.

THE WARRANT FOR THE PRESBYTERIAN VERSION OF THE PRAYER BOOK.

IN previous articles we have advocated these three means of correcting and improving our public worship:—1st. In all cases a careful attention to the rules and suggestions of the Directory; 2d. In many cases a system of services, with forms or examples, composed or compiled by the minister for his own assistance; 3d. In some cases, where the parties are so agreed, a liturgy, or scheme of common devotions, for both minister and congregation, containing not merely psalms and hymns, and Directory, but tables of Scripture lessons, forms of stated prayer, and of administration of the sacraments, and other rites of the Church. And in this concluding article, we desire now to show that either or all of these advantages can be secured in an edition of the Book of Common Prayer, as revised by the Royal Commission of Presbyterian divines, at the Savoy Conference, A. D. 1661, and in agreement with our Directory for Public Worship.

As this was with the writer no foregone conclusion, but a wholly unforeseen result of some studies and efforts in the direction of a truly Presbyterian liturgy, he begs the reader, who has followed him thus far, to candidly review the several historical facts upon which it is based, and the arguments upholding it.

1. *The Prayer-book was set aside for the Directory by the Westminster divines on avowed principles which admit of its resumption.* In their Preface, after recounting the evils then arising out of its forcible imposition upon the churches, they thus declared their motives:

"Upon these, and many the like weighty considerations, in reference to the whole Book in general, and because of divers particulars contained in it; not from any love to novelty, or intention to disparage our first reformers, (of whom we are persuaded that, were they now alive, they would join with us in this work, and whom we acknowledge as excellent instruments, raised by God, to begin the purging and building of his house, and desire they may be had of us and posterity in everlasting remembrance, with thankfulness and honor,) but that we may, in some measure, answer the gracious providence of God, which at this time calleth upon us for further reformation, and may satisfy our own consciences, and answer the expectation of other reformed churches, and the desires of many of the godly among ourselves, and withal give some public testimony of our endeavors for uniformity in Divine worship, which we have promised in our 'Solemn League and Covenant.' We have, after earnest and frequent calling upon the name of God, and after much consultation, not with flesh and blood, but with his holy word, resolved to lay aside the former liturgy, with the many rites and ceremonies, formerly used in the worship of God, and have agreed upon this following Directory for all the parts of public worship, at ordinary and extraordinary times."

We believe that both the spirit and the letter of these cautious declarations favor the point we are arguing. When it is remembered that the Directory was mainly a semi-political

device, resulting from the opposite forces of prelacy and independency, and that it utterly failed to secure the "covenanted
uniformity," for which it was orignally framed; and when it
is remembered that the objections therein enumerated against
the Prayer-book, such as the imposition of things indifferent as
terms of communion, the suppression of free prayer and
preaching, the obtrusion of new papistical ceremonies, and the
maintenance of an unedifying, beneficed clergy, were chargeable to the mere political and sectarian surroundings of the
Book, rather than to its contents, duly purged and amended;
and when, moreover, it is remembered that we, in this land
and age of greater light and freedom, are no longer harassed
by the untoward influences, and driven to the rash extremes,
which this liturgy then occasioned, and that all former difficul-
ties in regard to its use, in our present necessities and opportu-
nities, have subsided into mere inherited prejudices; we shall
surely not be inconsistent, to say the least, if we return to it
as to the work of our revered forefathers, and thereby again
illustrate our dearly bought liberty, as well to resume and
modify it, as to lay it aside according to the varying exigency
of times and occasions. And, lest it be thought we misrepre-
sent them, let the simple fact which afterwards followed be
next considered.

2. *The Prayer-book was actually revised by the framers of
the Directory, and their descendants, with a view to its resumption.* Among the Presbyterian Commissioners at the Savoy
Conference, were some of the most distinguished Westminster
divines;* their specimen of a "Reformed Liturgy" was taken
exclusively from the Bible, the Directory, and the Prayer-
book; and their own immortal writings still rank among our
standards of orthodoxy and piety. Both as scholars and theo-
logians they were unequalled, either then or since, and were
not despised even by their adversaries, who proffered them the
highest honors of that Church establishment which, with the
spirit of martyrs, they afterwards abandoned. It cannot be
charged, much less proved upon such men, that they were of a
compliant or compromising temper. While, as they declared,

* Tuckney, Calamy, Spurstow, Wallis, Case, Reynolds, Newcomen, Conant,
Lightfoot, etc.

4*

they had "not the least thought of depraving or reproaching the Book of Common Prayer," yet their "exceptions" against it were not only "general," but "particular" or verbal, with a degree of scrupulous minuteness that would now be deemed superfluous; and these "exceptions," having never been fairly acted upon by both parties, have come down to us without a trace or taint of concession. We have, in fact, all the materials of a thoroughly Presbyterian edition of the Prayer-book in the form of such historical documents as the following:

1. "The King's Warrant for the Conference at the Savoy."
2. "The Exceptions of the Presbyterian Ministers against the Book of Common Prayer," (including a written criticism upon both text and rubric, with proposed alterations, emendations, and additions.)
3. "The Answer of the Bishops to the Exceptions of the Ministers."
4. "The Petition for Peace and Concord, presented to the Bishops, with the proposed Reformation of the Liturgy."
5. "The Rejoinder of the Ministers to the Answer of the Bishops—the Grand Debate between the most Reverend the Bishops and the Presbyterian Divines, appointed by his sacred Majesty, as Commissioners for the Review and Alteration of the Book of Common Prayer, &c., being an exact account of their whole proceedings. The most perfect copy. London, 1661: pp. 1—148."*

The Book, as revised and amended by the aid of these documents, could not be chargeable with any private or modern fancies, but would embody the matured suggestions of learned and godly men, who were lawfully charged with the work of revision, and who, in that good work, endured great temptation and persecution. And the whole, besides being a worthy memorial of our Church forefathers, would be at least as truly Presbyterian as our present service-book, which contains a Directory of Worship, originally framed by ordained ministers of the Church of England, "with the assistance of Commissioners from the Church of Scotland,"† and a collection of hymns

---

* As collateral aids may also be used, the present English Prayer-book, with its Presbyterian emendations, for which the most reverend Bishops in their Preface thought fit to apologize; the proposed Prayer-book of 1689, which was framed in consultation with the leaders of the ejected Presbyterians, and which, in the opinion of Calamy, would have satisfied more than two-thirds of their number; and the different Presbyterian editions, dating before the Savoy Conference, especially the Second Book of King Edward VI., to which the Presbyterian Commissioners constantly appealed.

† Of the one hundred and twenty divines in the Westminster Assembly, five

compiled from all accessible sources. But the last shred of an objection, on the score of consistent Presbyterianism, must disappear before our next consideration.

3. As the Directory is but a skeleton of the Prayer-book, so the *Prayer-book itself is but a compilation which is more Presbyterian than Episcopalian in its sources.* We mean simply to say that, leaving out of view those portions which belong exclusively to neither party, but have been sanctioned and used by both, (being derived from ancient Christian liturgies, and from Lutheran formularies,) the remainder, which is by no means inconsiderable in character or quantity, is almost entirely Presbyterian. This is unquestionably true of the Book as it stood at the time of the Savoy Conference, and it is sufficiently true, for this argument, of the Book as it is now familiar to the American reader; as will appear by the following references, taken from Anglican authorities alone.

The Exhortation, General Confession, Declaration of Absolution, and General Thanksgiving, in the Order for Daily Prayer, and the Ten Commandments as they appear in the Ante-Communion Office, are admitted to be of Calvinistic origin.* All that remains (except the apocryphal Song and

---

were Commissioners from the Church of Scotland, six or seven were Independents, several were Episcopalians, and the remainder were English Presbyterians.

* It is generally conceded that these services, as used in the reformed churches, originated with Calvin, and were copied into the Anglican Church from his Strasburg Liturgy, as translated by his successor Pollanus, and by A. Lasko, both of whom were Calvinists and refugee pastors, with their congregations worshipping in England at the time the first Prayer-book was further reformed and amended. See History of the Prayer-book, by Archdeacon Berens, published by the Society for Promoting Christian Knowledge, pages 39, 41, 43, 87, 88, 141, 155—8; Archbishop Laurence's Bampton Lectures, p. 207—10; Freeman's "Principles of Divine Service," vol. I., p. 313; Proctor's Hist. of Prayer-book, pp. 48 and 49, note; "Private Prayers in the Reign of Queen Elizabeth;" Parker Society, p. 488, note; Strype's Eccl. Mem. Vol. II., p. 2, 33; Burnet's Hist. of Ref., p. 415; Strype's Life of Cranmer, p. 200, and Appendix; Heylin's Hist. of Ref., Pub. by Eccl Hist. Society, Vol. I., pp. 193, 226, 270, etc.

The General Thanksgiving was composed by Reynolds, one of the Presbyterian Commissioners at the Savoy Conference. See Proctor's Hist. of Prayer-book, p. 263, and authorities there quoted.

The Litany, when it differs from the ancient form, is in almost every instance taken from Bucer's translation. See any of the above writers.

The Epistles and Gospels were rendered in their present translation at the instance of the Presbyterian Commissioners. See as above.

Lessons,) viz., the Te Deum, the Litany, the Creeds, the Collects, Epistles, and Gospels, have passed from their ancient sources through Presbyterian sanctions, and under a Presbyterian revision, to their present form. In other words, the whole Lord's day service, as usually performed, contains but a single prayer* that can be traced to a distinctively Episcopalian origin; and for the obvious reason, partly, that that service was framed before the assertion of Prelacy against Presbytery arose, and also that its Protestant additions and emendations are almost exclusively from Calvinistic sources.

In the Occasional Offices of Baptism, Matrimony, Visitation of the Sick, and Burial of the Dead, the question of authorship lies between the Calvinist and the Lutheran, or between the French and the German Protestant, rather than between the Presbyterian and the Episcopalian. While portions of those formularies are clearly traceable to the Cologne liturgy of the Calvinistic† Bucer and Melancthon, yet, having thus originated outside of the pretentious Anglican Prelacy, they belong to the general class of Reformed or Protestant *non-*Episcopal rituals, and as such, might have continued in actual use, but for certain doubtful expressions and superstitious ceremonies, by which they were vitiated, and from which our ecclesiastical fathers in the Savoy Conference strove to purge them.

As to the Psalter, it is well known that it was first restored to the people, in the form of congregational psalmody, in the Church of Geneva, from whence it was copied, as a popular element of worship in the English churches.

Of the whole compilation, indeed, except the Ordinal or ordination services, and several political or State services, added after the Savoy Revision, it is safe to affirm, that were

---

* Even this exception is doubtful. The "Prayer for all Conditions of Men," by whomsoever composed, originated in the Presbyterian Revision, and was evidently modelled upon, if not largely quoted from, Calvinistic prayers, already authorized and domesticated in England. Compare Proctor's Hist. of Prayer-book, p. 262, with Liturgical Services Qn. Eliz., p. 266, and Eutaxia, pp. 157, 38, 39.

† Zurich Letters, 1st Series, pp. 161, 234. 2d Series, pp. 73, 120. Orig. Letters of Reformation, 488, 535, 544—548, 585, 688., Pub. by Parker Society. Calvin's Tracts, Vol. II., 281, 354—356, 496. Burnet's Hist. of Ref., p. 405.

it amended according to that revision, it would be as thoroughly Presbyterian in its historical sources as well as sanctions, and, in fact, in every thing but its present popular associations, as the book now used in our pulpits and pews. The almost universal impression to the contrary has arisen out of the false assumption that our forefathers were as much opposed to liturgy as Prelacy, or to the literary contents of the Prayer-book, as to the tyrannical and superstitious rites accompanying it. It is forgotten, or no longer known among us, that the Presbyterian Church in England, with her two thousand clergy, her scholars, divines, and patriots of illustrious memory, her prestige of learning, rank, and power, in the act of giving up, for conscience' sake, the high places and rich livings of an establishment which owed its restoration to her loyalty, also abandoned a liturgy to which her ministers had an hereditary right, upon which their adversaries were legally compelled to meet them in conference for their satisfaction, and which, at the same time, they declared they had "not the least thought of depraving or reproaching." And this hard alternative into which they were driven by the exigencies of a State religion, in an age of sectarian rancor and violence, we have thoughtlessly accepted and continued as our sole, normal condition. But surely, after two centuries of peaceful progress, in another country, under a government of equal laws, and in the midst of spontaneous tendencies towards a free, spiritual liturgy, it is high time to ask if there be not some safe mean between the wild extremes from which we have so happily escaped, and whether history has not reserved it as a just providential compensation, that we should now enter into the labors, while we vindicate the fame, of those faithful men " of whom the world was not worthy."

4. Our last and conclusive argument is, that the Prayer-book, thus revised, with our American Directory in place of the English Rubric, *is the only Presbyterian liturgy that is either desirable or practicable.* After what we have stated as to the origin and history of that compilation, we shall not now be suspected of any disloyalty in affirming that, with all its faults, it is simply incomparable. No one who studies the subject, historically and philosophically, can fail to see that it meets

the needs of ordinary divine service better than any other formulary that has ever been devised, or become widely prevalent. A fresh worker in this field, taking as his ideal of Christian worship a scheme of stated forms, which should express, in simple Scripture phrase, the common needs of a church assembly, and be redolent of the communion of saints in all lands and ages—such a worker, after all the thought and research he can bestow upon the question, at length finds that he has been anticipated by a book which is framed to fit the mould of the universal Christian heart, which is wrought out of the warp and woof of ancient and modern piety, which contains the cream of all liturgies, both of our own and of other churches, and which has lingering about it a savour of pure and fervent devotion belonging to no other uninspired composition. If he loves our English Bible, he must also love that English liturgy which was the product of the same age, and in the same sacred style. To attempt now any better devotional phraseology would be as vain as to frame a better version of the Holy Scriptures. To attempt any different compilation would be but to glean in fields already reaped and garnered; and to attempt any ingenious recomposition of its materials, would be but to incur the odium of imitation or invasion, where we ought rather to assert an original right of property and inheritance. It has, in fact, been the chief mistake of our liturgical writers hitherto, that, from a well-meant fear of concession or intrusion, they have so generally striven to ignore a collection which has been culled from the gathered wisdom and piety of the Church universal, and which, after all that has been said and done against it, has continued, for these several centuries past, the only Christian liturgy deserving the name.

We know very well, indeed, that as now viewed by Presbyterians, it has many serious blemishes and inconveniences, and even pernicious errors, the still remaining dross of the furnace through which it has passed; but none of these, it will be found, have escaped the searching revision and thorough expurgation of the Savoy divines, or need encumber it in the hands of those who are not trammelled with inflexible rubrics. As combined with a Directory, allowing to the minister his liberty to remedy, at discretion, the tedious length and multiplicity of its services, and neither requiring nor precluding responses, on the part of the congregation, nor indeed demanding any other behaviour than is already customary in our assemblies, it would, we honestly believe, be the best liturgy that could be desired, or now devised.

We will even go further, and declare our conviction that, as it is the only liturgy fit to be used, so it is the only one that can be used with any thing like Presbyterian consistency. The nature of our system, and the nature of the exigency, combine to shut us up to this alternative. On the one hand the wise, generous spirit of our system will not allow the whole Church to be hampered with any thing more liturgical than a Directory; and, on the other hand, the exigency to be met is such, that it cannot be fully supplied by mere private or voluntary efforts. For any single pastor to compose a liturgy, would be as absurd as to compose a hymn-book; and for him to compile one, exclusive of the Prayer-book, would be as impossible as to compile a new creed or psalter. No man or body of men now living could frame any better, or any other formulary, at all answering to the proper idea of a liturgy, than that which our ecclesiastical forefathers in England have first revised, and then bequeathed to us, invested with the halo of martyrdom; and by adopting it as the fruit of their orthodoxy, learning and piety, while we gain all the advantages of authority, antiquity, catholicity, and perfect fitness, we sacrifice neither our liberty, nor our just pride as Presbyterians.

Nor could its use in common with that highly respectable denomination, which meanwhile has arisen in our own country, and so faithfully preserved and honored it among us, be other than pleasing to any, in either Church, who "profess and call themselves Christians," or who are ready to rejoice at the many and great things in which Christians can agree, as compared with the few and small things in which they differ.

We conclude the whole subject with two inferences. The one is, that the liturgical question has already been exhausted, so far as discussion could exhaust it, by a former age. The time for mere argument has gone by. In these articles we have presented, not without some needful exaggeration, it may be, a side which we Presbyterians have but seldom viewed.

We know very well what strong reasonings can be brought from the opposite side; but we know also that no reasonings that could now be brought from either side would equal those of the disputants who were once so terribly in earnest, as to add battles to their books, diplomacy to their logic, and martyrdom to their orthodoxy.

The other inference is, that the whole question is one of the unsolved problems which the Old World has bequeathed to the New. Although so thoroughly canvassed there, yet it was at length settled only by the strong arm of the law, and in a manner that posterity here refuses to accept as final or satisfactory. The Directory of the Established Church of Scotland, and the Liturgy of the Established Church of England, the several fruits of a sectarian warfare, that would permit neither to live but by exterminating the other, cannot now be viewed, in the light of facts around us, as other than rash extremes, from which the free churches of this land are already verging towards a substantial unity, in the midst of trivial diversity.

On the 24th of August last, in the city of London, but out of the Church of England, was commemorated the bi-centennary of that black day in her saints' calendar, the second St. Bartholomew tragedy, which gave her the Prayer-book, without the pledged alterations, at a cost of so many martyrs for Presbyterian orthodoxy and spirituality. Should the same work as here issued on the basis of their revision, and in their name, do aught towards that spiritual "Act of Uniformity," which neither covenants nor statutes could then compel, or now retard, their testimony will not have been in vain.

WM. S. & ALFRED MARTIEN HAVE IN PRESS,

THE BOOK

OF

COMMON PRAYER,

AND ADMINISTRATION OF THE

SACRAMENTS,

AND

OTHER RITES AND CEREMONIES OF THE CHURCH,

AS REVISED BY THE

ROYAL COMMISSION OF PRESBYTERIAN DIVINES

AT THE SAVOY CONFERENCE, A.D., 1661,

AND IN AGREEMENT WITH

THE DIRECTORY FOR PUBLIC WORSHIP

OF THE

PRESBYTERIAN CHURCH IN THE UNITED STATES.

EDITED BY

CHARLES W. SHIELDS,

PASTOR OF THE SECOND PRESBYTERIAN CHURCH, PHILADELPHIA.

WITH AN APPENDIX,

CONTAINING THE DOCUMENTS OF THE PRESBYTERIAN REVISION, TOGETHER WITH
THE EDITOR'S EXPLANATORY NOTES AND REFERENCES.